Sports Illustrated KIDS

The Best of EVERYTHING

BASKETBALL BOOK

by Nate LeBoutillier

CAPSTONE PRESS
a capstone imprint

Sports Illustrated KIDS books are published by Capstone Press,
151 Good Counsel Drive, P.O. Box 669, Mankato, Minnesota 56002.
www.capstonepub.com

 Books published by Capstone Press are manufactured with paper
containing at least 10 percent post-consumer waste.

Library of Congress Cataloging-in-Publication Data
LeBoutillier, Nate.
  The best of everything basketball book / by Nate LeBoutillier.
     p. cm.—(All-time best of sports. Sports Illustrated kids)
  Includes bibliographical references and index.
  ISBN 978-1-4296-5468-5 (library binding)
  ISBN 978-1-4296-6327-4 (paperback)
  1. Basketball—Miscellanea—Juvenile literature. 2. Basketball—Records—Juvenile literature.
  3. National Basketball Association—Juvenile literature. 4. Basketball teams—United States—
  Juvenile literature. 5. Basketball teams—Ontario—Toronto—Juvenile literature. I. Title. II. Series.
  GV885.1.L42 2011
  796.323—dc22   2010038477

Editorial Credits

Anthony Wacholtz, editor; Tracy Davies, designer;
Eric Gohl, photo researcher; Eric Manske, production specialist

Photo Credits

AP Images/Paul Vathis, 44, 45 (t)
Corbis/Bettmann, 6
Dreamstime/Paskee, 56 (t)
Getty Images Inc./NBAE/Glenn James, 53 (t)
iStockphoto/Bill Grove, cover (background)
Library of Congress, 7, 9
Shutterstock/Aprilphoto, cover (basketball), 1; Diane Uhley, 10 (l); Sanderson Design, 10–11
Sports Illustrated/Al Tielemans, 13 (t), 15, 39 (tr); Andy Hayt, 33 (t); Bob Rosato, cover (bm), 4–5, 19 (b),
    24 (m & b), 30 (t), 31 (b), 40 (m), 48 (b), 49 (b), 57, 58 (t); Damian Strohmeyer, cover (bmr), 31 (t), 48 (t);
    David E. Klutho, 30 (b), 38 (t); Hy Peskin, 16, 26 (b), 40 (t); John Biever, 12, 25 (t & m), 35 (t), 53 (b),
    58 (b), 61; John D. Hanlon, 20 (t), 38 (b), 46, 47 (all), 51, 55 (b); John G. Zimmerman, 42 (m), 45 (b),
    54 (b); John Iacono, 21 (t), 54 (m); John W. McDonough, cover (tl, bl, br), 13 (b), 17 (b), 28 (all),
    29 (m & b), 31 (m), 35 (b), 37 (b), 39 (b), 40 (b), 41 (all), 49 (t), 59 (t & m); Manny Millan, cover (tr),
    17 (t), 18, 19 (t), 20 (b), 21 (b), 25 (b), 27 (t), 29 (t), 32, 33 (b), 34 (all), 36 (all), 37 (t), 39 (tl), 42 (t & b),
    43 (t & b), 50, 52, 54 (t), 55 (m), 58 (m), 59 (b), 60 (b); Richard Meek, 26 (t), 56 (b), 60 (t); Robert Beck,
    cover (bml), 43 (m); Simon Bruty, 22, 23 (all); Walter Iooss Jr., 8, 24 (t), 27 (b), 55 (t)

Printed in the United States of America in North Mankato, Minnesota.
092010   005933CGS11

TABLE OF CONTENTS

THE BEST OF BASKETBALL

"The invention of basketball was not an accident. It was developed to meet a need."

James Naismith

From the NBA and WNBA to the NCAA and the Olympics, basketball has continued to excite and entice fans all over the globe. The big-name players and fast-paced play keep the crowds coming back for more. From the time kids can dribble and shoot a basketball, they dream of playing in the spotlight like their favorite players. They strive to be able to shoot like Larry Bird and Ray Allen. They

work to box out and rebound like Wilt Chamberlain and Dwight Howard. They practice their ball handling skills so they can thread passes through defenders like John Stockton and Chris Paul.

Pro basketball has a rich history full of legendary players, coaches, and games. Take a look at the best the sport has to offer to see why it is one of the most popular sports in the world.

CHAPTER 1

BASKETBALL BIOGRAPHY

AMAZING FIRSTS

FIRST GAME

On December 21, 1891, physical education instructor James Naismith invented the game of basketball. He nailed a pair of peach baskets to the wall, about 10 feet (3 meters) off the floor at opposite ends of the room. Each team had three forwards, three centers, and three backs. The players tried to toss a soccer ball into their team's basket by passing the ball back and forth while eluding the defense. The ball couldn't touch the ground. The game consisted of two 15-minute halves and the first matchup ended in a 1-0 score.

JAMES NAISMITH

FIRST INTERCOLLEGIATE GAME

The first reported intercollegiate basketball game was played on the campus of Hamline University in St. Paul, Minnesota. The matchup was between the Hamline Porkers and the Minnesota State School of Agriculture on February 9, 1895. The Minnesota State School won the game 9-3.

FIRST PROFESSIONAL GAME

On November 1, 1946, the New York Knickerbockers took on the Toronto Huskies at Toronto's Maple Leaf Gardens. The visiting Knicks won the match 68-66.

FIRST WOMEN'S BASKETBALL TEAM

Senda Berenson, a teacher at Smith College in Northampton, Massachusetts, fielded the first women's team in 1893. Berenson made some modifications to the rules. She divided the court into three zones that the players could not leave. Violent actions, including snatching or batting the ball away from an opponent, were prohibited.

High school girls playing basketball in the early 1900s

FIRST MINORITY PRO PLAYER

Japanese-American point guard Wataru "Wat" Misaka was the first minority to play in the Basketball Association of America. He was only 5 feet 7 inches (170 centimeters), but he was lightning quick. He had led his college team at the University of Utah to NCAA and NIT championships. After serving in the U.S. Army, Misaka played three games for the New York Knicks in the 1947–1948 season. He scored seven points during his brief professional career.

BASKETBALL IN THE OLYMPICS

Basketball was first played as an Olympic sport in 1936 at the games in Berlin, Germany. Over the course of one week, 21 nations competed in a tournament-style play for the gold medal. The games were played outdoors on lawn tennis courts. The International Basketball Federation used the opportunity to test the effects of playing basketball professionally outdoors.

On the final day of the tournament, a heavy rainfall made it hard to bounce the ball, which limited the scoring. The United States won the gold medal game versus Canada by a score of 19-8. Joe Fortenbury of the U.S. led the game in scoring with seven points. Mexico matched up against Poland for the bronze medal, with Mexico winning the game 26-12.

The NBA's roots go back to the 1946–1947 season, when the Basketball Association of America started play with 11 teams. Over the next three seasons, four of the BAA's teams folded. Another league, the National Basketball League, joined with the BAA to become the National Basketball Association in 1949. However, another six teams folded the following year as the NBA struggled to gain momentum as a professional league. For almost a decade, the number of teams in the league dropped.

The NBA finally started to grow in 1961. The league added its first expansion team, the Chicago Packers, bringing the number of teams to nine. Bill Russell and the Boston Celtics won their sixth straight championship as a number of team dynasties emerged. The season brought amazing individual feats as well, including Wilt Chamberlain's 100-point game and Oscar Robertson's triple-double

average over the entire season. The NBA's growth took off from there until it became today's exciting 30-team league.

OSCAR ROBERTSON

THE FIRST TEAMS OF THE BAA (1946–1947)

WASHINGTON CAPITOLS

The Capitols had the best record (49–11), a great young coach in Red Auerbach, and three basketball stars: Bob Feerick, Fred Scolari, and Bones McKinney. They lost in the semifinals of the league's playoffs.

NEW YORK KNICKS

The winners of the league's very first game achieved a 33–27 season record. The Knicks are one of two BAA teams that have the same name today.

PITTSBURGH IRONMEN

The Ironmen had the league's worst record of 15–45. Press Maravich, father of NBA legend "Pistol" Pete Maravich, was a Pittsburgh reserve.

PHILADELPHIA WARRIORS

The Warriors' Joe Fulks was the league's top scorer, and coach Edward Gottlieb led the team to a 35–25 record. The Warriors defeated the Chicago Stags four games to one to win the BAA championship.

TORONTO HUSKIES

Big Ed Sadowski started the season as the Huskies' coach and most talented player, but he was traded after the team struggled early. Following the 1946–1947 season, the Toronto franchise disbanded.

PROVIDENCE STEAM ROLLERS

Guard Ernie Calverley drove the Steam Rollers to a 28–32 record while leading the league in assists. The next season Providence managed only a 6–42 record and folded after the following year.

BOSTON CELTICS

The team finished 22–38 in its first season, but the Celtics soon became a winning franchise. It is one of two BAA teams that still have the same name.

1946-1947 BOSTON CELTICS

CHICAGO STAGS

Stars Max Zaslofsky and Chick Halbert led the Stags to an impressive 39–22 record. They finished second in the playoffs behind the Philadelphia Warriors.

ST. LOUIS BOMBERS

Guard John Logan paced the Bombers to a fine 38–23 record. The team was topped two games to one by Philadelphia in the playoffs' opening round.

CLEVELAND REBELS

The Rebels finished with an even 30–30 record behind guard Frankie Baumholtz. They later obtained Big Ed Sadowski through a trade with Toronto.

DETROIT FALCONS

The Falcons were led by center Stan Miasek. The team finished with a 20–40 record and folded after its first and only season.

THE COURT

Pro basketball is a winter sport and is played indoors. The bounce of the basketball and the squeak of basketball shoes on the hardwood floor mix in with the cheers from the crowd. Most of the hardwood courts in the NBA are made of maple. They are coated with a protective material that prevents the wood from getting damaged.

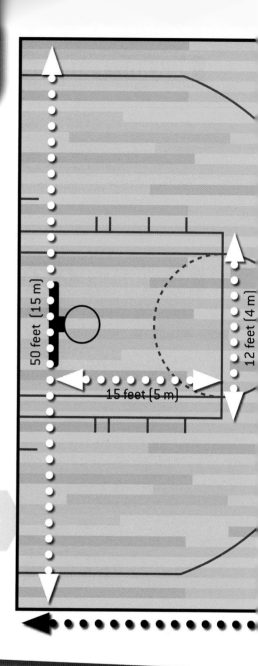

50 feet (15 m)

15 feet (5 m)

12 feet (4 m)

OTHER COURTS

The courts used in college basketball are slightly different from the courts in the NBA. Although the width of a college court is the same, they are 10 feet (3 meters) shorter. On a college court, the three-point line is about 3 feet (1 m) closer to the basket than in the NBA.

There are no specific court dimensions for outdoor courts, although they often resemble those of the NBA. The courts are usually made of asphalt or blacktop. These materials can withstand heat or water better than hardwood courts.

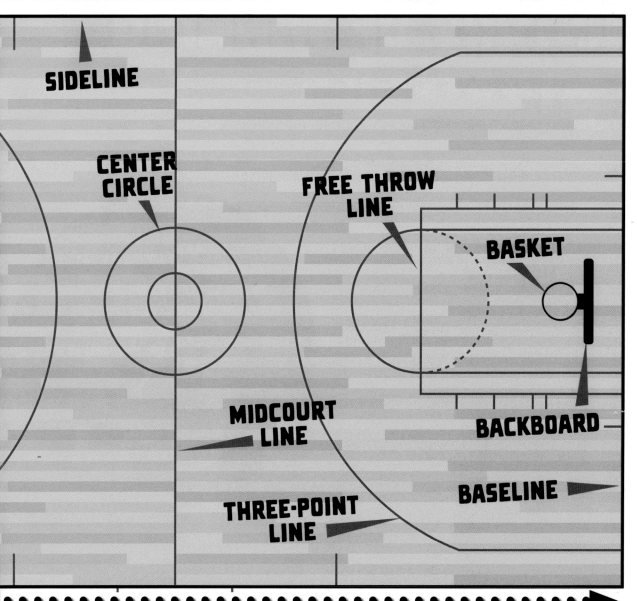

SIDELINE

CENTER CIRCLE

FREE THROW LINE

BASKET

MIDCOURT LINE

BACKBOARD

THREE-POINT LINE

BASELINE

94 feet (29 m)

POSITIONS

There are five players from each team on the court at all times:

point guard—player who brings the ball up the court and is a good passer

shooting guard—player who can shoot from the perimeter and is relied on for scoring

small forward—player who usually has the speed to play on the perimeter and the size to play in the post

power forward—player who spends most of the time in the post

center—player who is positioned near the basket; this player is often the tallest and biggest on the team

HISTORY OF WINNING STRATEGIES

MAN-TO-MAN DEFENSE

In a man-to-man defense, each defending player has a certain offensive player to guard. Most coaches throughout basketball's history have preferred this style of defense. Zone defense, a defense in which players are responsible for covering a certain area of the court, was accepted by the NBA in 2001.

MOTION OFFENSE

As far back as the 1920s, the Harlem Renaissance traveling basketball team was running a version of the motion offense. In this offensive strategy, the player passes the ball to a teammate, and then moves close to set a screen. Then the player cuts to the basket or jumps to the perimeter for a return pass. Legendary coach Hank Iba taught the motion offense at Oklahoma State from the 1930s through the 1960s. Bob Knight, who most famously coached at Indiana University, perfected the offense.

FULL-COURT PRESSURE

For teams with quick players or depth in their lineup, a full-court pressure defense is a great option. Whether playing man-to-man or zone, full-court pressure can force turnovers if offensive players are not used to being guarded while bringing the ball up the court. Full-court pressure is common in high school and college games, but pro teams rarely use it. By the time players hit the NBA, their dribbling and passing skills are highly developed, and the full-court press isn't as effective.

TRIANGLE OFFENSE

The triangle offense got its name from the triangular-shaped positioning of players who read each other's passes and cuts. College coach Sam Barry at the University of Southern California invented it in the 1940s. Coach Tex Winter at Kansas State University perfected the offense in the 1950s before it appeared in the NBA. The Chicago Bulls won six NBA titles in the 1990s with Winter assisting head coach Phil Jackson. When Jackson moved on to coach the Los Angeles Lakers, Winter and the triangle offense followed him to L.A, where they won another five championships.

PICK AND ROLL

Though the pick and roll offensive play was used for years, it became most popular in the NBA in the 1980s and 1990s. The pick and roll is a two-man play where one player sets a screen on the defender of the second player who has the ball. Then the screener rolls to the basket to receive a pass for a layup. John Stockton and Karl Malone worked this play to perfection for the Utah Jazz in the 1990s.

CHAPTER 2

TREMENDOUS TEAMS

AROUND THE NBA

There are 30 teams in the NBA—15 in the Eastern Conference and 15 in the Western Conference. The conferences are split into three divisions with five teams.

Sixteen teams, eight from each conference, make it to the playoffs. The winners from each conference play a best of seven series for the NBA title.

EASTERN CONFERENCE

ATLANTIC

Boston Celtics—The Celtics have retired 22 numbers and won 17 league championships in their team's history dating back to 1957

New Jersey Nets—The Nets made the NBA Finals in back-to-back seasons in 2002 and 2003 behind sweet-passing point guard Jason Kidd

New York Knicks—The two-time NBA champion Knicks play before passionate fans at Madison Square Garden

Philadelphia 76ers—Philadelphia's nickname has a historic connection; it comes from the Founding Fathers' signing of the Declaration of Independence in 1776 in Philadelphia

Toronto Raptors—Pro basketball returned to Toronto in 1995; the Toronto Huskies were a BAA founding team in 1946 but lasted only one season

CENTRAL

Chicago Bulls—The Windy City's pro team captured six NBA titles in the 1990s

Cleveland Cavaliers—Founded in 1970, the Cavaliers have often been a competitive team but have never won a championship

Detroit Pistons—The Pistons began in Fort Wayne, Indiana, where the team's owner, Fred Zollner, owned a piston-making company

Indiana Pacers—The Pacers hail from Indianapolis, home of the famous auto race, the Indianapolis 500; a pacer is a car that leads a parade of competing cars before the start of a race

Milwaukee Bucks—The Bucks have one NBA championship in their trophy case from the 1971 team, which featured Kareem Abdul-Jabbar and Oscar Robertson

SOUTHEAST

Atlanta Hawks—The Hawks started out in 1949 in the Tri Cities of Moline and Rock Island, Illinois, and Davenport, Iowa; the team landed in Atlanta in 1968

Charlotte Bobcats—The Bobcats opened for business in North Carolina in 2004; their predecessors, the Hornets, left the nest in Charlotte for New Orleans

Miami Heat—The Heat won its lone NBA title in 2005 behind Dwyane Wade and Shaquille O'Neal

Orlando Magic—In only their sixth season, the Magic made it all the way to the NBA Finals behind center Shaquille O'Neal

Washington Wizards—The Wizards won the NBA championship in 1978 as the Washington Bullets; they got their new name before the 1997–1998 season

WESTERN CONFERENCE

NORTHWEST

Denver Nuggets—The team got its name from the Colorado Gold Rush of 1859 that drew people to the Rocky Mountains

Minnesota Timberwolves—The Timberwolves nickname was one of two finalists; it beat out Polars when the team joined the NBA in 1989

Oklahoma City Thunder—The Thunder moved east to Oklahoma from Seattle, Washington, where they were called the SuperSonics

Portland Trail Blazers—Portland won its lone NBA title in 1977 behind Blazermania, the nickname for the Blazers' style of team play

Utah Jazz—The Jazz nearly won NBA titles in 1997 and 1998, finishing as runners-up twice to the Chicago Bulls

PACIFIC

Golden State Warriors—Before moving to San Francisco in 1962, the team was located in Philadelphia, where one of the team's best players, Wilt Chamberlain, was born

Los Angeles Clippers—In the California Gold Rush of 1849, many clipper ships sailed from South America to California ports; the port city of San Diego hosted the team before moving to LA in 1984

Los Angeles Lakers—Before moving to LA in 1960, the team played as the Minneapolis Lakers in Minnesota, a state containing thousands of lakes

Phoenix Suns—The Suns joined the NBA in 1968 and have made two NBA Finals appearances; they lost both times, in 1976 and 1993

Sacramento Kings—Before landing in Sacramento, the Kings played in Rochester, N.Y.; Cincinnati, Ohio; Omaha, Nebraska; and Kansas City, Missouri

SOUTHWEST

Dallas Mavericks—The leading scorer in Mavericks history is Dirk Nowitzki, the only German-born player to ever win the league's MVP Award

Houston Rockets—The Rockets got their start in San Diego in 1967 before moving to Houston, the home of NASA's Mission Control

Memphis Grizzlies—The Grizzlies were born in British Columbia, an area known for roaming grizzly bears; the franchise moved from Vancouver to Memphis in 2001

New Orleans Hornets—New Orleans lured the Hornets from Charlotte in 2002 after going without a basketball team for 22 years

San Antonio Spurs—Behind legendary big man Tim Duncan, the Spurs captured four NBA titles in the late 1990s and 2000s

Name the eight teams whose nicknames are animals.

Answer: Bobcats, Bucks, Bulls, Grizzlies, Hawks, Hornets, Raptors, Timberwolves

DYNASTIES BY THE DECADE

MINNEAPOLIS LAKERS OF THE 1950s

With a BAA title in 1948–1949 and four NBA titles in the first five years of the 1950s, the Minneapolis Lakers became basketball's first dynasty. Center George Mikan led the charge for the Lakers. Other team greats included forwards Jim Pollard and Vern Mikkelsen, and coach John Kundla.

BOSTON CELTICS OF THE 1960s

Possibly the most dominant dynasty pro basketball has ever seen, the Celtics won every title in the 1960s except in 1967. The team featured many great players, including Hall of Famers Bob Cousy, Bill Russell, Tom Heinsohn, K.C. Jones, Sam Jones, Bill Sharman, John Havlicek, Frank Ramsey, and Tom Sanders. Legendary coach Red Auerbach took the reins of the dominant franchise.

Bob Cousy splits the defense on a fast break.

LOS ANGELES LAKERS AND BOSTON CELTICS OF THE 1980s

The 1980s belonged to Magic Johnson's Lakers and Larry Bird's Celtics. The two teams combined to win eight of the 10 NBA Finals that decade. The dueling franchises made up the best rivalry in NBA history.

Magic Johnson (far right) uses his teammate's screen to break free.

UCLA BRUINS OF THE 1970s

Though the University of California, Los Angeles Bruins played college ball, they looked like a pro team in the late 1960s and 1970s. Centers Lew Alcindor (who later changed his name to Kareem Abdul-Jabbar) and Bill Walton manned the post. Behind coach John Wooden, UCLA won 10 NCAA championships in 12 seasons from 1964 to 1975. From 1971 to 1974, the Bruins were unstoppable, winning 88 consecutive regular-season games.

CHICAGO BULLS OF THE 1990s

The Bulls won three consecutive titles in the 1990s two separate times (1991–1993 and 1996–1998). Guard Michael Jordan led the way, with sidekick Scottie Pippen doing damage from his forward position and coach Phil Jackson manning the bench.

LOS ANGELES LAKERS AND SAN ANTONIO SPURS OF THE 2000s

Kobe Bryant and Shaquille O'Neal helped the Lakers win the first three titles of the 2000s. Bryant led the Lakers to two more titles in 2009 and 2010. The San Antonio duo of Tim Duncan-David Robinson was devastating against Spurs' opponents as they made title runs in 1999 and 2003 before Robinson retired. Duncan then teamed with guards Tony Parker and Manu Ginobili for titles in 2005 and 2007.

Kobe Bryant (right) drives against David Robinson (center) and Tim Duncan.

DREAM TEAM

The United States Olympic Committee decided to use professional basketball players for the 1992 Olympics instead of only amateurs as it had before. This created the possibility for the formation of the best team in the history of basketball. The names glittered like gold on paper before the team even began play.

After losing the gold medal to the Soviet Union in South Korea in 1988, the new Team USA was ready to bring home the gold in the 1992 Olympics. What followed was blowout after blowout as Team USA —labeled the "Dream Team"—rocked the courts in Barcelona, Spain. The team was so dominant that its average margin of victory was 43.8 points per game. The team ran so smoothly that Coach Chuck Daly never called a time-out during the entire tournament.

"It was like Elvis and the Beatles put together," said Daly. "Traveling with the Dream Team was like traveling with 12 rock stars. That's all I can compare it to."

1992 TEAM USA ROSTER

Michael Jordan	Charles Barkley	Patrick Ewing
Magic Johnson	Clyde Drexler	Chris Mullin
Larry Bird	David Robinson	John Stockton
Karl Malone	Scottie Pippen	Christian Laettner

IN IT TO WIN

In the years it has participated, the U.S. men's basketball team has failed to win the Olympic gold medal only three times since 1936: 1972 in Munich, Germany; 1988 in Seoul, South Korea; and 2004 in Athens, Greece.

USA's Dwyane Wade and Argentina's Manu Ginobili fight for a loose ball during the 2004 Olympics.

BEST TEAMS

1971-1972
LOS ANGELES LAKERS

69–13 in regular season, 12–3 in playoffs,
NBA Champions

Coach: Bill Sharman
Starting Five:
Jerry West (25.8 points per game, 9.7 assists per game)
Gail Goodrich   (25.9 ppg)
Jim McMillian   (18.8 ppg)
Happy Hairston   (13.1 ppg, 13.1 rebounds per game)
Wilt Chamberlain   (14.8 ppg, 19.1 rpg)

The Lakers streaked to 33 straight regular-season wins and a 31–7
mark on the road—both NBA records that still stand today.

GAIL GOODRICH (25)

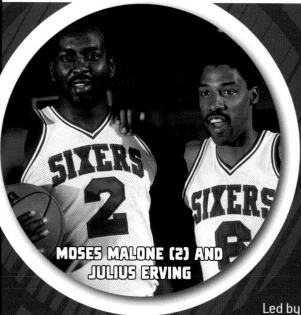

**MOSES MALONE (2) AND
JULIUS ERVING**

1982-1983
PHILADELPHIA 76ERS

65–17 in regular season, 12–1 in playoffs,
NBA Champions

Coach: Billy Cunningham
Starting Five:
Maurice Cheeks   (12.5 ppg, 6.9 apg)
Andrew Toney   (19.7 ppg, 4.5 apg)
Julius Erving   (21.4 ppg)
Marc Iavaroni   (5.1 ppg)
Moses Malone   (24.5 ppg, 15.3 rpg)

Led by the dominant Malone, the Sixers romped through the
playoffs, losing just a single game on the way to the best
playoff winning percentage (.923) in NBA history.

1985-1986 BOSTON CELTICS

67–15 in regular season, 15–3 in playoffs, NBA Champions

Coach: K.C. Jones
Starting Five:
Dennis Johnson   (15,6 ppg, 5.8 apg)
Danny Ainge   (10.7 ppg, 5.1 apg)
Larry Bird   (25.8 ppg, 9.8 rpg, 6.8 apg)
Kevin McHale   (21.3 ppg, 8.1 rpg)
Robert Parish   (16.1 ppg, 9.5 rpg)

The team with one of the best records in the franchise's 17 NBA Championship history rolled over the competition with selfless teamwork and playmaking.

1986-1987
LOS ANGELES LAKERS

65–17 in regular season, 15–3 in playoffs, NBA Champions

Coach: Pat Riley
Starting Five:
Magic Johnson (23.9 ppg, 12.2 apg, 6.3 rpg)
Byron Scott   (17.0 ppg)
James Worthy   (19.4 ppg, 5.7 rpg)
A.C. Green   (10.8 ppg, 7.8 rpg)
Kareem Abdul-Jabbar   (17.5 ppg, 6.7 rpg)

The Lakers bested the Boston Celtics in the most competitive NBA Finals in the history of the game.

MAGIC JOHNSON

1995-1996 CHICAGO BULLS

72–10 in regular season, 15–3 in playoffs, NBA Champions

Coach: Phil Jackson
Starting Five:
Michael Jordan   (30.4 ppg, 6.6 rpg, 4.3 apg)
Ron Harper   (7.4 ppg)
Scottie Pippen   (19.4 ppg, 6.4 rpg, 5.9 apg)
Dennis Rodman   (5.5 ppg, 14.9 rpg)
Luc Longley   (9.1 ppg)

Jordan returned from his baseball experiment to help the Bulls take the NBA by storm. His first full season back, Chicago set the league record for the best regular season in NBA history.

MICHAEL JORDAN

THE HARLEM GLOBETROTTERS

Since 1926 the Harlem Globetrotters have toured the world playing a fan-oriented brand of basketball. Entrepreneur Abe Saperstein managed the team in its early days as the team went on the road to play exhibition games. At first all of the team's players were African-Americans from Chicago. At the time neither college basketball nor most semi-pro leagues allowed black people to play.

Harlem Globetrotters' Rocket Rivers lays it in against the Generals.

In a typical Globetrotters game, the team builds a quick lead. Then the players start clowning around and toying with the opposition. Globetrotter players are experts in fancy dribbling and sleight-of-hand passing, as well as trick shots. But their skills on the court are always at a professional level. In 1948 and 1949, the Globetrotters took on the Minneapolis Lakers—the top pro team at the time—and beat them.

After African-American players were integrated into college and pro ball in the 1950s and 1960s, the talent pool for the Globetrotters started to dry up. But they were still able to attract enough talent to keep their show on the road. In addition, they occasionally hired NBA players during the players' offseason.

Ant Atkinson shows off his skills after a dunk.

Special K Daley (21) splashes a referee and the crowd during a break in the game.

The Harlem Globetrotters' signature song is "Sweet Georgia Brown," a tune made famous by Ben Bernie and his Hotel Roosevelt Orchestra in 1925. The jazzy song was re-recorded by Brother Bones and His Shadows in 1949. It features a whistling melody and snapping beat that the Globetrotters play before games begin. The players stand in a circle and throw tricky passes to each other as the tune plays in the background.

FACT:

The Harlem Globetrotters have retired the jersey numbers of five players in their history: Wilt Chamberlain's 13, Marques Haynes' 20, Meadowlark Lemon's 36, Reece "Goose" Tatum's 50, and Curly Neal's 22.

BEST COLLEGE PROGRAMS

UNIVERSITY OF CALIFORNIA, LOS ANGELES

Bruins basketball would never be the same after John Wooden became the UCLA coach in 1948. He won 10 championships over 12 years during the 1960s and 1970s. This amazing feat put UCLA in the record books as one of the most dominant dynasties basketball has ever seen.

Notable Alumni: Jamaal Wilkes, Lew Alcindor (Kareem Abdul-Jabbar), Bill Walton

JOHN WOODEN

DUKE UNIVERSITY, 2010

DUKE UNIVERSITY

Mike Krzyzewski, the coach of the Blue Devils since 1980, stirred up a basketball powerhouse when he landed at Duke. As NCAA champions four times—with another 11 appearances in the Final Four—Duke possesses an unmatched modern-day trophy case.

Notable Alumni: Johnny Dawkins, Bobby Hurley, Christian Laettner, Grant Hill

UNIVERSITY OF KENTUCKY

One of the oldest basketball programs in the country originated at the University of Kentucky. The Wildcats were playing organized ball as far back as 1902. The team prospered under legendary coach Adolph Rupp in the 1940s, and it remains a powerhouse today with an impressive seven NCAA titles.

Notable Alumni: Pat Riley, Dan Issel, Jack "Goose" Givens

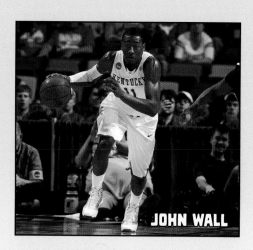

JOHN WALL

UNIVERSITY OF KANSAS

The first coach in school history was James Naismith, the inventor of the game of basketball. Following Naismith, coach Phog Allen provided direction for the Jayhawks and helped organize the NCAA and its national tournament. KU's distinguished program remains competitive today, last winning a national championship in 2008.
Notable Alumni: Wilt Chamberlain, Danny Manning

UNIVERSITY OF KANSAS, 2008

UNIVERSITY OF NORTH CAROLINA

UNC is a basketball giant. The Duke-North Carolina rivalry is one of the greatest in college basketball. Dean Smith coached the Tar Heels from 1961 to 1997 and retired as the coach with the most wins in NCAA history.
Notable Alumni: Larry Brown, James Worthy, Michael Jordan

2009 NCAA CHAMPIONS

INDIANA UNIVERSITY

The Hoosiers play basketball in possibly the most hoops-crazy state in the nation. Passionate coach Bob Knight led the Crimson and Cream to the last undefeated college basketball season in modern history when IU went 32–0 in 1975–1976.
Notable Alumni: Scott May, Isiah Thomas, Steve Alford

BOB KNIGHT

CHAPTER 3

PRIME-TIME PLAYERS

LEGENDS IN NBA HISTORY

1950s

The first big man to star in a pro basketball game was center George Mikan. He was so dominant in college at DePaul University in the mid-1940s that he caused the NCAA to make goaltending illegal. Mikan led the Minneapolis Lakers to titles in 1949, 1950, 1952, 1953, and 1954. Another 1950s great was Bob Cousy, who defined the point guard position with his wizardlike ball-handling and passing skills for the Boston Celtics.

BILL RUSSELL

1960s

The 1960s belonged to centers Bill Russell and Wilt Chamberlain. In every year of the decade, either Russell or Chamberlain was the starting center on the championship team. Russell's Boston Celtics won nine of those 10 titles. The postseason often brought excitement because Russell took on Chamberlain in the playoffs many times. Another outstanding player in the 1960s was Oscar Robertson. He was an athletic guard for the Cincinnati Royals who contributed in many categories.

BOB COUSY

1970s

Guard Jerry West's Los Angeles Lakers were great in the 1960s, but they had a tough time winning an NBA championship. They finished second a frustrating seven times over that span. But the Lakers finally made their breakthrough in 1972, winning the title behind the play of the sharpshooting West. Center Kareem Abdul-Jabbar and his skyhook helped the Bucks to Milwaukee's lone franchise title in 1971. After Abdul-Jabbar was traded to the Lakers in 1975, he won five more championships and went on to become the NBA's all-time leading scorer.

1980s

The 1980s belonged to point guard Magic Johnson of the Lakers and forward Larry Bird of the Celtics. Magic's Lakers won five titles and Bird's Celtics won three during the decade. Magic's clutch playmaking and Bird's smooth shooting and passing made them legends and increased the NBA's popularity by leaps and bounds.

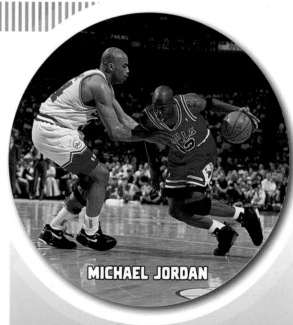

MICHAEL JORDAN

1990s

There is no question who was basketball's king in the 1990s. Guard Michael Jordan led his Chicago Bulls to six championships in the decade with unmatched skills and style. The Bulls might have won more titles if the high-scoring Jordan hadn't left the NBA for nearly two seasons in the middle of the decade to try his hand at professional baseball.

LARRY BIRD

SUPERSTAR GUARDS

Guards bring the ball up the court and dish out incredible passes, drive the lane, or step back to knock down a three-pointer. They are known for running the offense and being great ball handlers. These guards have highlighted the NBA over the last decade.

Chris Paul

Height	6 feet (183 cm)
Weight	175 pounds (79 kg)
Team	Hornets
Points	6,668
Assists	3,446
Steals	822

In just five seasons, Chris Paul has led the league in assists twice and in steals three times.

Dwyane Wade

Height	6 feet 4 inches (193 cm)
Weight	212 pounds (96 kg)
Team	Heat
Points	11,967
Assists	3,126
Steals	862

Dwyane Wade led the league in scoring during the 2009-2010 season.

Jason Kidd

Height	6 feet 4 inches (193 cm)
Weight	205 pounds (93 kg)
Teams	Mavericks, Suns, Nets
Points	16,142
Assists	10,923
Steals	2,343

Jason Kidd is also a fierce rebounder, making him a constant triple-double threat.

Steve Nash

Height	6 feet 3 inches (191 cm)
Weight	195 pounds (88 kg)
Teams	Suns, Mavericks
Points	14,771
Assists	8,397
Steals	776

A threat from behind the arc, Steve Nash has 3,439 career three-pointers.

Kobe Bryant

Height	6 feet 6 inches (198 cm)
Weight	200 pounds (91 kg)
Team	Lakers
Points	25,790
Assists	4,766
Steals	1,554

Kobe Bryant has led the league in scoring four times and has made 12 All-Star appearances.

*Stats are through the 2009–2010 season.

FORWARDS & CENTERS

From Dirk Nowitzki's ability to hit the trey to Dwight Howard's monstrous dunks, the big men of the NBA have a variety of talents. With a mix of veterans and rising stars, the league features a highlight reel of forwards and centers.

LeBron James

Height	6 feet 8 inches (203 cm)
Weight	240 pounds (109 kg)
Teams	Cavaliers, Heat
Points	15,251
Rebounds	3,861
Blocks	482

LeBron James has 3,810 assists and 955 steals to round out his impressive stats.

Kevin Durant

Height	6 feet 9 inches (206 cm)
Weight	215 pounds (98 kg)
Team	Thunder
Points	5,967
Rebounds	1,453
Blocks	212

Up-and-coming superstar Kevin Durant led the league in scoring in 2009–2010.

Kevin Garnett

Height	6 feet 11 inches (211 cm)
Weight	220 pounds (100 kg)
Teams	Timberwolves, Celtics
Points	22,267
Rebounds	12,188
Blocks	1,790

Kevin Garnett is a regular at the All-Star Game, making 13 appearances over 15 years.

Dirk Nowitzki

Height	7 feet (213 cm)
Weight	237 pounds (108 kg)
Teams	Mavericks
Points	21,111
Rebounds	7,802
Blocks	936

Dirk Nowitzki can shoot from a distance, with 2,977 career three-pointers.

Dwight Howard

Height	6 feet 11 inches (211 cm)
Weight	240 pounds (109 kg)
Team	Magic
Points	8,538
Rebounds	6,189
Blocks	1,042

In his first six seasons in the NBA, Dwight Howard led the league in rebounds five times.

*Stats are through the 2009–2010 season.

GREATEST RIVALRY

MAGIC VS. BIRD

If you're looking for the greatest matchup basketball has ever seen, look no further than Magic Johnson versus Larry Bird. The rivalry played out on the college court for the first time in the NCAA championship game of 1979. The matchup continued in the NBA regular season, and three times in the NBA Finals. Beyond that, it was played out in television commercials, video games, and in the imaginations of youngsters on playgrounds, in driveways, and on Nerf hoops in living rooms everywhere.

FACT:

Magic Johnson and Larry Bird each won the MVP Award three times—Bird in 1984, 1985, and 1986, and Magic in 1987, 1989, and 1990.

Magic Johnson

Games: 906	Minutes Played: 33,245
Points: 17,707	Rebounds: 6,559
Assists: 10,141	Steals: 1,724
Blocks: 374	Threes: 325
FG%: .520	FT%: .848

Earvin "Magic" Johnson grew up in the 1960s and 1970s. He played basketball in Michigan and landed a sports scholarship at Michigan State University. Larry Bird played basketball in small-town Indiana before landing at Indiana State University. Their differing playing styles were showcased when Michigan State and Indiana State faced off in the 1979 NCAA Championship. Magic was a freewheeling point guard with a flashy smile and game to match. Bird was a quiet shooter who was a clutch performer with a steady game.

Magic and Michigan State bested Bird and Indiana State for the NCAA title in the most-watched college game in basketball history. Then the two took their rivalry to the pros. Magic joined the Los Angeles Lakers and led his team to the 1980 NBA title as a rookie. Bird joined the Boston Celtics and led them to a title the next season. Every season but two in the 1980s, a Magic- or Bird-led team took the title. Magic and Bird faced off in the NBA Finals three times in the 1980s.

After competing for so many years, the two players became friends. "We got this connection that's never going to be broken. I mean, right to our graves," said Bird, years after his retirement. "They will be talking about this 100 years from now."

Larry Bird

Games: 897	Minutes Played: 34,443
Points: 21,791	Rebounds: 8,974
Assists: 5,695	Steals: 1,556
Blocks: 755	Threes: 649
FG%: .496	FT%: .886

BEST DUNKERS

MICHAEL JORDAN

"Air" Jordan was possibly the best dunker of all time. With his tongue out and arm cocked, Jordan was a threat to dunk on any player at any time.

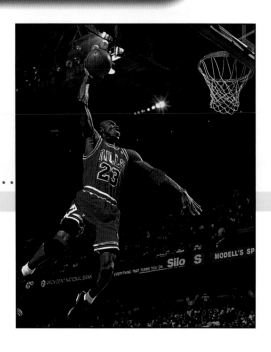

DOMINIQUE WILKINS

When "The Human Highlight Film" rocked the rim, the entire arena felt it. One of the hardest dunkers in NBA history was a joy to watch for Hawks fans in Atlanta.

SHAWN KEMP

The "Reign Man" made his mark with the Seattle SuperSonics, dunking in ways that few big men before him had ever dreamed.

VINCE CARTER

Vince Carter shocked the world when he leaped over—yes *over*—7-foot-2-inch (218-cm) center Frederic Weis of France in the 2000 Olympics.

DARRYL DAWKINS

The jams of "Chocolate Thunder" were not only beautiful—they were dangerous. Two shattered backboards are the legacy of the 6-foot-10-inch (208-cm), 260-pound (118-kg) Philadelphia 76ers star.

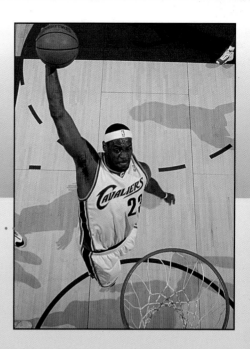

LEBRON JAMES

"King" James combines size—6 feet 8 inches (203 cm), 240 pounds (109 kg)—with unbelievable athleticism that enables him to leap high and throw down in spectacular fashion.

JULIUS ERVING

One of the pioneers of dunking showmanship, "Dr. J" thrilled 76ers fans in Philly for years with his many high-flying "house call" jams.

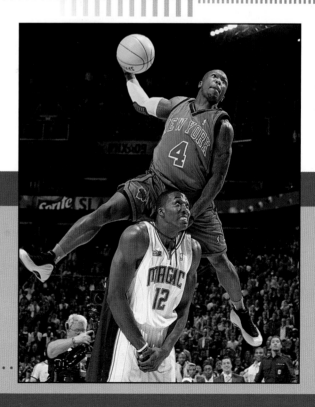

NATE ROBINSON

At 5 feet 9 inches (175 cm), Nate Robinson is arguably the best short dunker in the NBA. The three-time NBA Dunk Contest champion (2006, 2009, and 2010) boasts a 44-inch (112-cm) vertical leap.

SIGNATURE MOVES

KAREEM ABDUL-JABBAR'S SKY HOOK

Shot with either hand effectively, Kareem Abdul-Jabbar's skyhook was as graceful as a swan and virtually unstoppable.

JULIUS ERVING'S HOUSE CALL

Nothing would fire up a crowd like watching Dr. J deliver a House Call. Julius Erving would glide down the court, cup the ball in his right wrist, swoop into the air, and throw the ball through the hoop in a graceful slam.

GEORGE GERVIN'S FINGER ROLL

"The Iceman" perfected one of the prettiest shots in the NBA. George Gervin's long arms and huge hands enabled him to flip in finger rolls with the lightness of a raindrop.

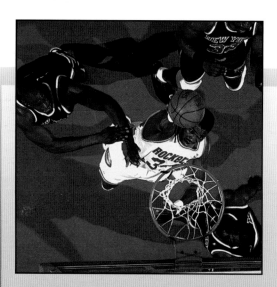

HAKEEM OLAJUWON'S DREAM SHAKE

Hakeem Olajuwon loved to receive the ball in the post. He would fake one way, extending the ball out with one hand to entice his defender to steal it. He would then spin back the opposite direction for a layup or dunk.

MICHAEL JORDAN'S FADEAWAY

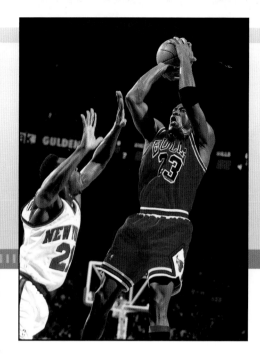

"Air" Jordan's age eventually limited his dunking ability, but he had perfected another unguardable move. Jordan's spinning fadeaway jump shot separated him from his opponent and usually found the net.

JOHN STOCKTON TO KARL MALONE PICK AND ROLL

Few people could set harder screens than Karl Malone. When John Stockton zipped around the screen, Malone would roll to the basket and receive a pass for the slam.

TIM HARDAWAY'S KILLER CROSSOVER

Tim Hardaway easily made his defenders look foolish and clumsy with his crossover. He would yo-yo the ball from his right hand to his left before dribbling it back to his right as he exploded to the hoop.

SHAQUILLE O'NEAL'S DROP AND DUNK

Immovable as a mountain, Shaquille O'Neal tortured his opponents by simply taking one backward step to the basket, turning, and hammering down a jam.

BEST NICKNAMES

"THE HUMAN ERASER"

Marvin Webster was one of the best shot blockers in the game during the 1970s and 1980s.

"THE MAILMAN"

Karl Malone, a muscular scorer and rebounder for the Utah Jazz, could be counted on to deliver with the game on the line.

"DR. DUNKENSTEIN"

Though measuring only 6 feet 4 inches (193 cm), guard Darrell Griffith of the Utah Jazz spent much of his time in the 1980s playing above the rim.

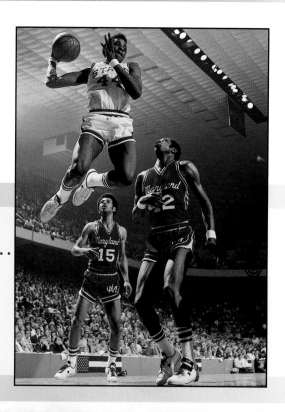

"SKYWALKER"

With an amazing 4-foot (122-cm) vertical leap, David Thompson seemed to walk on air as he went in for a slam dunk.

"THE ROUND MOUND OF REBOUND"

Forward Charles Barkley was a big man who could block and tear down rebounds with the best of them.

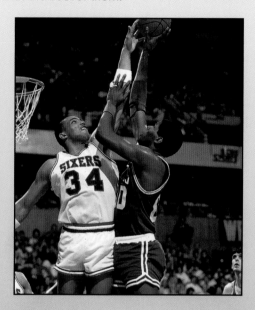

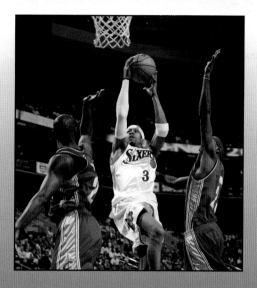

"THE ANSWER"

If Philadelphia 76ers fans were questioning whether their team could find a way to win, Allen Iverson often had the answer for them in the 1990s and early 2000s.

TRIVIA

Can you match the nickname to the player?

1. The Big Dipper	Kevin Garnett
2. The Big Ticket	Elvin Hayes
3, Human Highlight Reel	Bill Milkvy
4. AK 47	Willis Reed
5. The Dunkin' Dutchman	Oscar Robertson
6. The Owl Without a Vowel	Wilt Chamberlain
7. Houdini of the Hardwood	Rik Smits
8. The Big O	Bob Cousy
9. The Big E	Andrei Kirilenko
10. The Captain	Dominique Wilkins

ANDREI KIRILENKO

Answers: 1. Wilt Chamberlain, 2. Kevin Garnett, 3. Dominique Wilkins, 4. Andrei Kirilenko, 5. Rik Smits, 6. Bill Milkvy, 7. Bob Cousy, 8. Oscar Robertson, 9. Elvin Hayes, 10. Willis Reed

GREATEST COACHES

RED AUERBACH

Red Auerbach made his mark in 16 seasons with Boston. He helped redefine the game by emphasizing teamwork and cooperation. He coached the Celtics to a record-setting nine championships before moving up to the front office.

PHIL JACKSON

Phil Jackson set the record for most NBA titles won as a coach with 10 in 2009. He has coached NBA greats Michael Jordan and Scottie Pippen with the Bulls, and Shaquille O'Neal and Kobe Bryant with the Lakers. A creative motivator, Jackson is considered one of the best at managing rosters filled with both ego and talent.

DON NELSON

"Nellie" was one of the true innovators of the game, unafraid to experiment with cutting edge strategies that opponents refer to as "Nellie Ball." In 2009–2010 Don Nelson became the NBA coach with the most career wins with 1,335. Nellie also had a fine playing career, and his number 19 jersey was retired by the Boston Celtics.

PAT RILEY

Pat Riley won four titles coaching the "Showtime" Lakers in the 1980s. He later had a successful run coaching the Knicks in the 1990s before moving to Miami and guiding the Miami Heat to its only championship in 2005. He holds the record as the only coach to take three different teams to the NBA Finals. Riley drew praise for building up his teams' endurance by working them hard in practice.

JERRY SLOAN

After 11 seasons as a player in the NBA, Sloan turned to coaching. At the end of the 2009–2010 season, Sloan had coached the Utah Jazz for a record-setting 22 straight seasons. Although Sloan has yet to win a title, the Jazz reached the NBA Finals in 1997 and 1998. He has a career record of 1,190–780.

LENNY WILKENS

Lenny Wilkens was one of the first people to be elected to the Hall of Fame as both a player and a coach. He played and coached for four of the same teams (Hawks, Sonics, Cavaliers, and Trail Blazers). He also coached the Raptors and Knicks. When he retired from coaching in 2005, Wilkens had set the record for most coaching wins with 1,332.

CHAPTER 4

REMARKABLE RECORDS

Scoring

1. Kareem Abdul-Jabbar	38,387
2. Karl Malone	36,928
3. Michael Jordan	32,292
4. Wilt Chamberlain	31,419
5. Julius Erving	30,026

Kareem Abdul-Jabbar also tops the minutes played list with 57,446.

Rebounds

1. Wilt Chamberlain	23,924
2. Bill Russell	21,620
3. Moses Malone	17,834
4. Kareem Abdul-Jabbar	17,440
5. Artis Gilmore	16,330

Bill Russell was inducted into the Hall of Fame in 1975.

Assists

1. John Stockton	15,806
2. Jason Kidd*	10,923
3. Mark Jackson	10,334
4. Magic Johnson	10,141
5. Oscar Robertson	9,887

Jason Kidd is a 10-time All-Star.

Blocks

1. Hakeem Olajuwon	3,830
2. Dikembe Mutombo	3,289
3. Kareem Abdul-Jabbar	3,189
4. Artis Gilmore	3.178
5. Mark Eaton	3,064

In 1989–1990 Hakeem Olajuwon became one of five players to get 375 blocks in a single season.

Steals

1. John Stockton	3,625
2. Michael Jordan	2,514
3. Gary Payton	2,445
4. Jason Kidd*	2,343
5. Maurice Cheeks	2,310

John Stockton stole the ball 263 times during the 1988–1989 season.

Threes

1. Reggie Miller	2,560
2. Ray Allen*	2,444
3. Dale Ellis	1,719
4. Peja Stojakovic*	1,703
5. Jason Kidd*	1,662

With his smooth shot, Reggie Miller also led the league in free-throw percentage five times.

*still active; stats through 2009–2010 season

43

THE 100-POINT GAME

In a performance for the ages, Wilt Chamberlain scored 100 points in a single game on March 2, 1962. Chamberlain, who was also known as "The Big Dipper" and "Wilt the Stilt," tallied the amazing amount for the Philadelphia Warriors. The Warriors won the game 169-147 against the New York Knickerbockers.

The game was played in Hershey, Pennsylvania. It was an alternative home game site for the Warriors, who were trying to attract more fans in the region by branching out. Chamberlain achieved his remarkable record by scoring 23 points in the first period, 18 in the second, 28 in the third, and 31 in the fourth. He made 36 of 63 shots from the field and went 28 for 32 from the free-throw line.

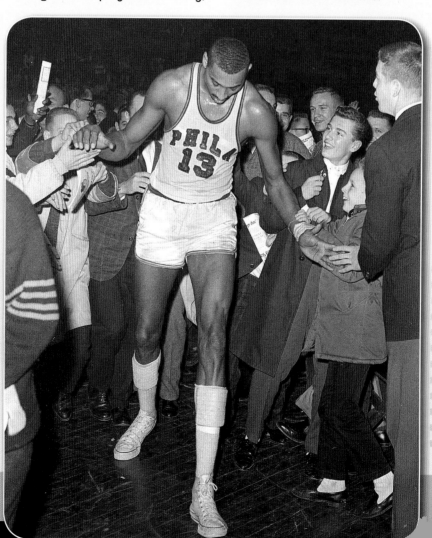

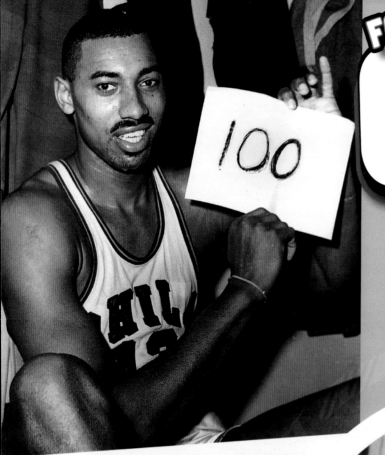

The only other pro players to score more than 70 points in a single game are Kobe Bryant (81 points, 2006), David Thompson (73 points, 1978), Elgin Baylor (71 points, 1960), and David Robinson (71 points, 1994). Chamberlain scored 70 points or more six times in his career.

"As time goes by, I feel more and more a part of that 100-point game," Chamberlain said, years later. "It has become my handle, and I've come to realize just what I did."

The 100-point game was just the beginning for Chamberlain. He played 11 more seasons after the legendary game, reaching amazing career totals in points (31,419) and field goal percentage (.520). He was a rebounding machine, averaging more than 20 rebounds per game in 10 of his 14 seasons. He is the all-time rebounding leader with 23,924. He also tops the list for career minutes per game with 45.8, and he is fifth with 47,859 total minutes played.

THIRTY-THREE IN A ROW

In 1971 the Los Angeles Lakers were poised to make their move for the NBA title. After the franchise moved from Minneapolis to LA in 1960, the Lakers had been to the NBA Finals seven times, only to be defeated every time. The Lakers of 1971–1972 were on a mission.

JIM MCMILLIAN

After the first nine games of the season, the Lakers' record stood at 6–3, and aging superstar forward Elgin Baylor decided to retire. In his place, forwards Jim McMillian and Happy Hairston added a spark to the team's other three stars, sharpshooting guards Jerry West and Gail Goodrich, and do-it-all center Wilt Chamberlain. In their 10th game of the season, the Lakers won 110-106 against the Baltimore Bullets. That victory started a 33-game win streak that lasted until the Milwaukee Bucks beat them 120-104 on January 9, 1972. The streak shattered the previous record of 20 straight wins set by the Bucks the previous season.

Guided by first-year coach Bill Sharman, the Lakers coasted to a record-breaking 69–3 regular season mark. They breezed through the opening rounds of the playoffs before facing the New York Knicks in the Finals. Though the Lakers lost Game 1, they rebounded to win the next four games. The Lakers won their first NBA championship trophy since moving to Los Angeles—the perfect ending to a marvelous season.

JERRY WEST

WILT CHAMBERLAIN

FACT:

The most consecutive losses during a single NBA season is 23, set by two franchises: the Vancouver Grizzlies of 1995–1996 and the Denver Nuggets of 1997–1998. The Cleveland Cavaliers dropped an all-time record 24 games straight over two seasons from 1981 to 1982.

CHAPTER 5

FAN FAVORITES

BEYOND FUNDAMENTALS

KOBE BRYANT

ALLEY-OOP

To perfect an alley-oop, you need a pinpoint passer and a high-flying dunker. Most often performed at the end of a fast break, the passer lofts a soft pass near the rim for a high-flying teammate to dunk it home. Famous alley-oopers include brothers Al and Gerald Tucker at Oklahoma Baptist University in the 1960s and David Thompson and his guards at North Carolina State in the early 1970s. Magic Johnson and Greg Kelser of Michigan State University flashed many alley-oops for the fans in the late 1970s.

FACT:

Brian Taylor of the San Diego Clippers was the leader in three-point field goals in 1979–1980, the first season the NBA adopted the three-point shot. Taylor, a graduate of Princeton University, led all NBA players with 90 three-pointers in 239 attempts, a success rate of 38 percent. The all-time leader for three-pointers made in a season was Ray Allen. He made 269 of 653 shots (41 percent) for the Seattle SuperSonics in 2005–2006.

RAY ALLEN

NO-LOOK PASS

SHAWN MARION

On a fast break, the best way to confuse the defenders is by dishing out a no-look pass. As the ball-handler looks one way, the defense is fooled as the pass heads in the opposite direction to an open teammate. Magic Johnson of the Los Angeles Lakers perfected the no-look pass, and he recognized the discipline it took to become a great ball-handler. "I practiced all day," Johnson said of his childhood training. "I dribbled to the store with my right hand and back with my left. Then I slept with my basketball." Today many young guards in college and the pros try to copy the magic of Johnson's no-look pass.

THREE-POINTER

The team is losing, and the clock is winding down. What's the fastest way to catch up? Three-pointers! To become great three-point shooters, players practice making shots from farther and farther away from the hoop. The three-point shot was introduced into professional basketball in 1961 with the formation of the American Basketball League, which lasted only one full season. The ABA adopted a three-point shot when it started in 1967, and the NBA followed in 1979. The popularity of three-pointers rose thanks to long-range bombers such as "Downtown" Freddie Brown and Larry Bird. College basketball adopted the three-point shot in 1986, and high school leagues followed soon after.

JOE JOHNSON

Julius Erving (6) drives the baseline against two Lakers defenders.

THE DOCTOR'S GOT MOVES

The Philadelphia 76ers were battling the Los Angeles Lakers in Game 4 of the 1980 NBA Finals. In the fourth quarter 76ers forward Julius "Dr. J" Erving drove the baseline. When two Lakers defenders moved in to stop him, Erving jumped into the air, swooped under the basket—almost out-of-bounds—and laid the ball up and in on the other side. Said Lakers guard Magic Johnson, "I thought, 'What should we do? Should we take the ball out, or should we ask him to do it again?' It's still the greatest move I've ever seen in a basketball game, the all-time greatest."

STEAL OF A GAME

The Boston Celtics held a one-point lead against the Philadelphia 76ers during Game 7 of the 1965 Eastern Conference Finals. The 76ers were looking to inbound the ball and try for one last shot to win the game and head to the NBA Finals. During the inbounds pass, Celtics forward John Havlicek batted the ball away from the defender for a legendary steal. The play was described with much emotion by Celtics broadcaster Johnny Most: "[76ers guard Hal] Greer is putting the ball in play. … He gets it out … and Havlicek steals it! Over to Sam Jones. Havlicek stole the ball! It's all over! It's all over! Johnny Havlicek is being mobbed by the fans. It's all over! Johnny Havlicek stole the ball!"

EITHER HAND

Larry Bird of the Boston Celtics was playing in his first NBA Finals in 1981. During Game 1 he amazed his teammates, the opposing Houston Rockets, and the Boston Garden crowd. He took an outside shot from the right wing but saw that the shot was going to fall short. He followed his shot, and as the ball bounded off the rim, Bird jumped into the air for the rebound in his right hand. As he fell out of bounds, he switched the ball to his left to flip it in the hoop. "I've never seen anything like it," said Celtics general manager Red Auerbach. "It was just a magnificent play."

CAPTAIN COMEBACK

During the 1970 playoffs, New York Knicks center and team captain Willis Reed was injured. He was expected to miss Game 7 of the 1970 NBA Finals against the Los Angeles Lakers. But just before tipoff, Willis appeared to the delight of Knicks fans at Madison Square Garden. He scored the game's first two baskets and led the Knicks to a rout. "When Willis came out onto the court, it was like the place exploded," said Knicks forward Bill Bradley. "Chills were going up and down everyone's spines."

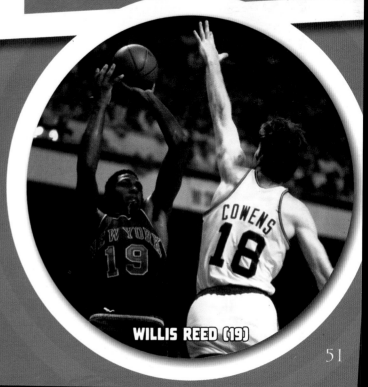

WILLIS REED (19)

CLUTCH PERFORMANCES

1970 NBA FINALS, GAME 3: LOS ANGELES LAKERS VS. NEW YORK KNICKS

The Knicks led 102-100 with time running out, but Lakers guard Jerry West canned a shot from 10 feet (3 m) behind the half-court line to send the game into overtime. Had the shot counted for three, the Lakers would've won the game, but the three-point shot was still years away in the NBA. Despite West's heroics, the Knicks won in overtime, 111-108.

1986 NBA WESTERN CONFERENCE FINALS, GAME 5: HOUSTON ROCKETS VS. LOS ANGELES LAKERS

With one second remaining, Rockets center Ralph Sampson received an inbounds pass. He made an amazingly difficult backward flip shot to win the game 114-112, sending Houston to the NBA Finals.

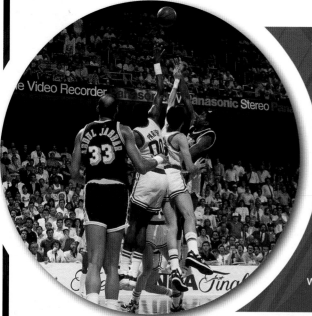

1987 NBA FINALS, GAME 4: LOS ANGELES LAKERS VS. BOSTON CELTICS

With less than five seconds remaining and the Lakers down 106-105, Magic Johnson hit a "Junior Sky Hook" over two Celtics defenders to win the game. The shot was similar to Lakers center Kareem Abdul-Jabbar's own deadly Sky Hook. "You expect to lose on a sky-hook," said Celtics star Larry Bird. "You don't expect it to be from Magic." The Lakers went on to win the NBA Championship.

1995 NBA EASTERN CONFERENCE SEMIFINALS, GAME 1: INDIANA PACERS VS. NEW YORK KNICKS

With the Pacers down 105-99 and only 18 seconds remaining, Pacers guard Reggie Miller went on a tear. He hit two three-pointers and a pair of free throws to help his team steal the game away from New York, 107-105.

1997 NBA WESTERN CONFERENCE FINALS, GAME 6: UTAH JAZZ VS. HOUSTON ROCKETS

The Jazz had endured 11 consecutive seasons of losing in the playoffs, and 1997 was a new season. In Game 6 of the Western Conference Finals, guard John Stockton nailed a jumper from deep on the left wing as time expired. Having won the game and the series against the Houston Rockets, Utah went on to play in its first NBA Finals.

John Stockton (12) makes the game-winning jump shot.

1998 NBA FINALS, GAME 6: CHICAGO BULLS VS. UTAH JAZZ

With the Chicago Bulls down 86-83 and less than a minute remaining, the series looked like it would go to seven games. Michael Jordan came to the rescue with three straight clutch plays. He hit a tough driving shot, and then he stole the ball from Utah's best player, Karl Malone. He finished with a jump shot with five seconds remaining to seal the title with an 87-86 Bulls win.

BEST QUOTES

"It's one thing to hear about it from your coach, but when your wife tells you it stinks, you tend to work on it."

—Orlando Woolridge (NBA player, 1981–1994), on a flaw in his game

"I asked him, 'Son, what is it with you? Is it ignorance or apathy?' He said, 'Coach, I don't know and I don't care.'"

—Frank Layden (Utah Jazz coach, 1981–1989), about a former player

"I don't create controversies. They're there long before I open my mouth. I just bring them to your attention."

—Charles Barkley (NBA player, 1984–2000), explaining why he often got into trouble

"Am I in a beauty contest or something? I wasn't put on this earth to look good or impress anybody."

—Doug Moe (Denver Nuggets coach, 1980–1990), defending his sloppy sideline wardrobe

"Everybody pulls for David, nobody roots for Goliath."

—Wilt Chamberlain (NBA player, 1959–1973)

"If you're a basketball player, you've got to shoot."

—Oscar Robertson (NBA player, 1960–1974) · · · · ·

"We can't win at home. We can't win on the road. I just can't figure out where else to play."

—Pat Williams (front office executive for the Philadelphia 76ers and Orlando Magic), commenting on the Magic's 17–27 record during the 1992–1993 season

"Right up until the time I retired at age 37, I felt like there were still things I could do better."

—Julius Erving (NBA player, 1971–1987) · · · · ·

"I knew it was time to retire when I was driving down the lane and got called for a three-second violation."

—Johnny "Red" Kerr, (NBA player, 1954–1966; coach, 1966–1970; and announcer, 1975–2008)

"Sport is the only profession I know of that when you retire you have to go to work."

—Earl Monroe (NBA player, 1967–1980) · · · · ·

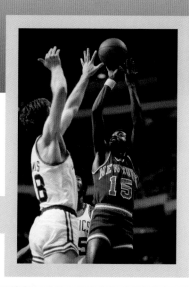

BEST ARENAS

With thousands of screaming fans clapping their hands and stomping their feet, you can feel the energy coursing through the gym during a close game. Some arenas have become legendary because of their history, the players, and even the fans.

BOSTON GARDEN

The Boston Garden opened in 1928 and was built with boxing matches in mind. Soon it became home to one of the best pro basketball teams. In the 1960s the Celtics racked up title after title. Larry Bird and the boys won three more titles on the Garden's famed parquet floor in the 1980s. The run ended when the arena was demolished in 1997.

MADISON SQUARE GARDEN

When it opened in 1968, Madison Square Garden was the fourth version of the arena. The Knicks won championships there in 1970 and 1973. But the Garden has also hosted the New York Rangers' pro hockey team and St. John's University athletics. The arena has even hosted professional wrestling, the Ringling Brothers and Barnum & Bailey Circus, the Westminster Kennel Club Dog Show, and both the Democratic and Republican national conventions.

RUCKER PARK

Rucker Park in New York City's borough of Manhattan was named for noted Harlem teacher Holcombe Rucker, who started basketball tournaments in the park for underprivileged children. "The Rucker" became known as the place to play pick-up basketball in the 1960s. NBA greats such as Julius Erving, Kareem Abdul-Jabbar, and Nate Archibald all found their match at Rucker after the NBA season ended.

CONSECO FIELDHOUSE

The home of the Indiana Pacers in Indianapolis is a modern marvel built in a retro style. Opened in 1999, the arena combines Indiana basketball history and architecture with contemporary additions such as luxury boxes, wide concourses, and up-to-date technology.

ROSE HILL GYMNASIUM

The oldest college basketball arena still in use opened in 1925 on the campus of Fordham University in the Bronx, New York. The gym played host to the final high school game of Lew Alcindor in 1965.

CAMERON INDOOR STADIUM

The Cameron Indoor Stadium opened on the Duke University campus in 1940 and was designed by architect Julian Abele, who studied at the Ecole des Beaux Arts in Paris. The Durham, North Carolina, arena houses one of the most boisterous fan bases in college basketball—the Cameron Crazies. Duke students hoping to score seats in the arena camp out on the lawn nearby.

HOOPS STYLE

HEADBANDS

Guard Slick Watts of the Seattle SuperSonics and center Bill Walton of the Portland Trail Blazers began wearing headbands in the early 1970s. Watts used his to keep the sweat out of his eyes. Walton wore one to secure his hair to his head. Modern-day players such as Carmelo Anthony (right) continue to wear headbands, although some admit it's strictly a fashion statement.

KNEE PADS/BRACES

Knee braces were first used to support sore or surgically repaired knees. But some players, such as New York Knicks center Patrick Ewing (left), began wearing knee pads for extra protection. Other players, such as the Chicago Bulls' Michael Jordan and Scottie Pippen, wore knee braces on their calves as a fashion accessory.

WRISTBANDS

Rick Barry was one of the first NBA players to wear wristbands. He used them to wipe away sweat from his eyes. Later, players such as Reggie Miller of the Indiana Pacers wore larger wristbands that covered most of the forearm. Horace Grant of the Chicago Bulls and Ben Wallace (right) of the Detroit Pistons added sweat bands around their biceps.

SHOES

Shoes started off in canvas and rubber. Converse Chuck Taylor All-Stars or Pro Keds were the rage in the 1960s and 1970s, before Adidas and Nike offered popular leather high tops in the late 1970s and 1980s. By the 1990s players wanting to wear the best could purchase Nike's "Air Jordan" shoes. Modern players can make thousands or even millions of dollars per year in sneaker endorsements.

UNIFORMS

Basketball uniforms were once made of tight polyester, and included belts and long socks or leggings. In the 1990s, thanks in part to Michael Jordan, shorts grew longer and jerseys became baggier. Uniform fonts and colors have also changed throughout the decades, though trends in the 2000s have seen styles go retro.

LeBron James sporting the retro Cavs jersey

FACT:

Hairstyles change with each new fashion trend, and basketball players' hair has been no different. But the hairstyles of colorful forward Dennis Rodman of the Chicago Bulls in the mid-1990s gave new definition to the term "fashion." He would often sport a new hairstyle every week that ranged from leopard print to pink to multicolored.

TIMELINE
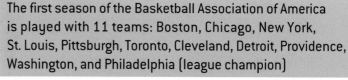

1946–1947	The first season of the Basketball Association of America is played with 11 teams: Boston, Chicago, New York, St. Louis, Pittsburgh, Toronto, Cleveland, Detroit, Providence, Washington, and Philadelphia (league champion)
1949–1950	The National Basketball Association begins with 17 teams
1954	The Minneapolis Lakers, led by center George Mikan, win their fifth title
1960	The Boston Celtics repeat as NBA champions with a win over the St. Louis Hawks; the win is the second of a streak of nine titles in the 1960s
1967	The American Basketball Association is founded and competes alongside the NBA
1969	At age 22, Wes Unseld of the Baltimore Bullets becomes the youngest player to win the MVP Award
1972	The Los Angeles Lakers roll to the NBA title after setting a league record with a 33-game winning streak during the regular season

1980	Celtics forward Larry Bird wins Rookie of the Year honors; another rookie, guard Magic Johnson, leads the Lakers to the NBA title and wins the Finals MVP
1986	Larry Bird wins his third straight MVP, tying a record with Bill Russell and Wilt Chamberlain
1990	The Detroit Pistons capture the second of back-to-back titles behind the play of Isiah Thomas and Joe Dumars
1992	Magic Johnson returns for the mid-season All-Star Game despite being HIV positive and treats fans to a memorable MVP performance
1995–1996	The Chicago Bulls set the league record with 72 regular season wins and become NBA champions

1997	The Women's National Basketball Association begins play with eight teams: Charlotte Sting, Cleveland Rockers, Houston Comets, New York Liberty, Los Angeles Sparks, Phoenix Mercury, Sacramento Monarchs, and Utah Starzz
1999	The San Antonio Spurs win their first NBA title behind the twin towers, David Robinson and Tim Duncan
2003	The Cleveland Cavaliers win the NBA Lottery and select homegrown talent LeBron James with the first pick in NBA Draft
2008	The Boston Celtics win their 17th NBA title—tops among NBA franchises—behind the play of their Big Three: Paul Pierce, Ray Allen, and Kevin Garnett
2010	The Los Angeles Lakers win the NBA championship to tie Boston for a league-leading 17 franchise titles

Match the current NBA team with its original home.

1. Golden State Warriors	San Diego, California
2. Sacramento Kings	Charlotte, North Carolina
3. Washington Wizards	Rochester, New York
4. Utah Jazz	Vancouver, British Columbia, Canada
5. Philadelphia 76ers	Seattle, Washington
6. Houston Rockets	Syracuse, New York
7. Memphis Grizzlies	Philadelphia, Pennsylvania
8. Oklahoma City Thunder	Chicago, Illinois
9. New Orleans Hornets	New Orleans, Louisiana

Answer: Warriors—Philadelphia; Kings—Rochester, Wizards—Chicago; Jazz—New Orleans, 76ers—Syracuse; Rockets—San Diego, Grizzlies—Vancouver, Thunder—Seattle, Hornets—Charlotte

GLOSSARY

CENTER: position of a player who plays mostly near the basket; this player is often the tallest and biggest on the team

CLUTCH: describes a player who performs well during crucial moments of the game

FORWARD: position of a player who plays both inside and outside; the players in this position are often skilled at scoring on offense in a variety of ways

GOALTENDING: when a defensive player stops the ball from going in the hoop after the ball has started to descend during a shot; a goaltending call results in a basket for the offense

GUARD: position of a player who plays mostly on the perimeter; this player is often one of the quicker players on the team who can dribble and pass well

PAINT: the rectangular area marked by a large rectangle directly under the basket and extending to the free-throw line; the area is often painted a different color from the rest of the court

POINT GUARD: type of guard who brings the ball up the court and is a good passer

POST: the area around the basket, generally within a 10-foot (3-m) radius, where the center or forwards try to get open to receive a pass

POWER FORWARD: type of forward who spends most of the time in the post and is usually next in size behind the center

SCREEN: a play where an offensive player tries to block a defender so that a teammate can break free from the defender; also called a pick

SHOOTING GUARD: type of guard who can shoot from the perimeter and is relied on for scoring

SIGNATURE: describes a style of play or specific move that a player is known for

SMALL FORWARD: type of forward who is balanced in scoring, defending, and passing; the small forward usually has the speed to play on the perimeter and the size to play in the post

TRIPLE-DOUBLE: reaching double figures in three categories in a single game

READ MORE

Doeden, Matt. *The World's Greatest Basketball Stars.* Mankato, Minn.: Capstone Press, 2010.

Fawaz, John. *High-Flying Stars.* New York: Scholastic Inc., 2007.

Kaufman, Gabriel. *Basketball in the Big Ten Conference.* New York: Rosen Central, 2008.

Rappoport, Ken. *Basketball's Top 10 Slam Dunkers.* Berkeley Heights, N.J.: Enslow Publishers, 2010.

Shea, Therese. *Basketball Stars.* New York: Children's Press, 2007.

INTERNET SITES

FactHound offers a safe, fun way to find Internet sites related to this book. All of the sites on FactHound have been researched by our staff.

Here's all you do:

Visit www.facthound.com

Type in this code: 9781429654685

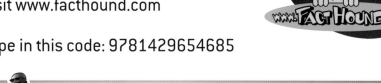

Check out projects, games and lots more at
www.capstonekids.com

INDEX